Also by Toni Thomas:

Chosen
Fast as Lightening
Walking on Water
Blue Halo
Ace Raider of the Unfathomable Universe
You'll be Fast as Lightening Coveting my Painted Tail
Hotsy Totsy Ballroom
Love Adrift in the City of Stars
In the Pink Arms of the City
In the Kingdom of Longing
The Things We Don't Know
In the Boarding House for Unclaimed Girls
They Became Wing Perfect and Flew
Unburdened Kisses
Bandits Come and Remove Her Body in the Night
There is This
Here
The Smooth White Vanishing
Perishing in the Rain
A Different Measure of Moonlight
The Secret Language of River
Inside Her a River of Snow was Traveling
Paradise on a Shoestring
The Arbiter of Her Own Flame

A Bride of Amazement

First published in 2025 by Annalese Press
West Yorkshire HD9 3XZ
England

Copyright © 2009 Toni Thomas

All rights reserved. No part of this publication may be reproduced, stored, or transmitted in any form, or by any means electronic, mechanical or photo-copying, recording or otherwise, without the express written permission of the publisher.

Cover design and layout by Peter Wadsworth
La Communiante, Bastien-Lepage, 1875

British Library Cataloguing-in-Publication Data
A catalogue record for this book is available on request from the British Library.

ISBN 978-1-0685744-3-6

Acknowledgments

With appreciation to the following presses for selecting these poems, or a version for publication -

"My Father Accumulates Hope" *Pennine Platform* (UK)

"We live Five Blocks from the Swansea Sweater Mill" *Struggle*

"My Father Speaks in Consolation" *Vallum* (Canada)

"If my mother had a predilection for sin" *Peregrine #26*

"My Father Wears a Kilt" *Willow Review*

"My Father Puts No Store in the Sheer Nylon" *Purple Patch* (UK)

"My Father Has a Hunch the World Will Not Save Him" *Green Mountain Review*

"I ask you to cure my lover's lips" *Pulsar Poetry* (UK)

"You are Raking the Fields" *Deronda Review*

"You never reduce me" "You ask your army of ants" *Bloodroot Literary Magazine*

"You Uncrank Your Voice" *Studio* (Australia)

For Julian
whose love was
always as wide and generous
as the sky of dawn opening.

Contents

Part One *We Never Eat Ordinary Bread*

In the book of your love	3
You hold your hands like birds mating	4
Woodland children	5
Provocation	6
Anteater	7
You gather the mute	8
It is Lent	9
Broken valentines	10
The clover's burning	11
Yellow canary	12
The weight of things	13
Lunar New Year	14
Sermon	15

Part Two *When the Sumac Arrives On My Lips*

Famine	19
Sacrifice	20
Tease	21
Your vows	22
Longing	23
When *You Make My Heart Swoon*	24
Pulpit	25
Suction cup	26
Altar	27
On a clear day	28
Spotless	29
We send our prayers upward	30

Come autumn	31
Epistle	32
In a bid to please you	33
You threaten	34
Fallen cathedral	35

Part Three *The Tyrant of Black Beetles*

You swallow the crow	39
You wear your brown beret	40
You go around in cutoffs	41
Grey flannel	42
A preacher in worn shoes	43
You bolt the house shut	44
Hail Marys	45
Father	46
I am unable to understand	47
Back then	48
Hydrant of psalm	49
Stranger	50
Blue chastening	51
Ringing	52
Premature bride	53
My father trophies the dead	54

Part Four *The Sky's Least Certain Homilies*

Half sung prayer book	57
Torn places	58
It was the moment of shot gunned glass	59
You wear your bangle hat	61
You tire of plaguing your head	62

If you were a young girl	63
I was wax winging	64
My mother	65

Part Five *You Want to be a Troubadour*

A troubadour	69
Kisses	70
There is the promise of spring	71
Devotion	72
An inventor	73
In my dream	74
It is hard to believe	75

Part Six *You Ask the Dark to Speak*

When they amputate your bad leg	79
In the hospital	81
Levitation	82
New bread	83
When we ward off	84
Your heart is a cobbled mill	85
You wear a kilt	86

Part Seven *The Afterbirth of Attrition*

When your sumac grazes my lips	89
The chef in a pampered kitchen	90
You usher my life	91
You run a brew pub for love	92
Hymn	93
You stockpile kisses	94
Pulpits	95

Part Eight *A Chorus of Varied Thrush in the Trees*

Snow	99
You send juncos into the tree	100
I used to shrink inside	101
A shy being	102
You make room	103
You wear your lusty carnation	104
Epistle of light	105
Aerial	106
You stop being oracular	107
If I can't say goodbye	108
Easter Lily	109

Part Nine *She Crowds Honeysuckle Into the Pale of My Days*

Since her burial	113
My mother had a predilection for kisses	114
I want to help	115
If my mother	116
I make a shrine	117
Exiled	118
My mother hairpins hope	119

Part Ten *The Flock of Birds in My Bed*

Come April	123
My father wants to preside	124
I was once the product	125
My father has divorced himself	126
When his sketchy past	127

Pear trees	128
Grapes	129
Secrets	130
You worship	131
The coral barrettes	132
Yellow carnations	133
Formosa	134
Pampering	135
Consolation	136
It was not how I thought it would be	137
You speak in the retinol of birds	138

When it's over, I want to say: all my life
I was a bride of amazement.
I was the bridegroom taking the world
into my arms.
      Mary Oliver

The gods give, like twin flowers,
power and rain, memory and oblivion.
      Gabriela Mistral

I had to cross the solar system
before I found the first thread of my red dress.
I sense myself already.
Somewhere in space hangs my heart,
shaking in the void, from it streams sparks
into other intemperate hearts.
      Edith Södergran

Part One

We Never Eat Ordinary Bread

In the book of your love

I slide into a white dress
study the rain
bird's august sanctuary

wear my days sodden
the resolution of field grass
to hold to its roots.

In the book of your love
I spin with possibility
let the missing rehearse
their sorrows in me.

But are some seasons
calamity
poverty forced to drink
from shame's cup?

You hold your hands like birds mating

In the old country they would say
you *made a good birth*
are the red prairie
eye of dawn opening
provocation to welcome
what is least earned.
No tar pitch muddies your path
prevents the rain from cleansing.

I navigate by the light of your gaze
stand atop the wing tip of your shoes
till the past won't speak dirty.

Your hands are spring rain
banked epistles
slow blooming crocus
stay glued like smooth stockings
to perfectly planed legs.

Woodland children

You wrap gum
into care packages
send them out
a sermon against vice.

Their hard substance
turns putty in my mouth
a balloon
stretched river

till I can almost
hem back trees
anoint my past with
no swear words

rise up
into the swell of paradise
we're told waits
pregnant
pert as a princess.

Provocation

You travel mercy, live by it
inspire me to take what I have
make a home
crimson wedded to ochre
coal to ivory
till I am more than
the unsung prophecy
tilted house.

But if poverty forswears me
as her bride
what will I do
when the rains come?

Anteater

You gobble ants
termites
tether the hard edged past
to the weight of your hymns.

Your willing apprentice
I want to be worthy
of the space you hold
in your heart

am coated in rapt imperialism
the troubadour ardor
of your lips.

You gather the mute

the departed
the sawn in half woman
turn suet into soufflé
rust into eggs
hold immigrant sun
Polish nuns dancing.

I want to avenue your surplus
not scuff my knees
in bog country
while the women weep.

It is Lent

You ask me to rise up
forget the gilded vocabulary
attest to the original measure
of my birth.

It is Lent
the time of fasting
when you will grow lean
as a birch tree

when my mother will keep watch
smooth like good linen
the tired folds of your shirt.

Broken valentines

Your lonely hearts club
gathers the faint, the bruised
sunken lullaby
invents a new fit.

I comb hair, dab my lips
in the crimson of your
voice's jukebox

become purple pigment
stained and swamped
with the wash of your fruit

become the risen body
after the wake

spit and wipe
work hard to rub soft
the peril of you.

The clover's burning

Even if I wound my life
with the heft of your chorus
we live on your words like some
people live on streaky bacon
the promise of a second home
become thick icing
an aerial landscape
turn the field, back seat of our car
into chapel.

Are you my original lover
last resort
when the world wields hardballs
when I am left to sink or paddle
in an iced river
pretend I am not terrified
of what is about
to become of us?

Yellow canary

You scold the yellow canary
in our neighbor's back yard
lecture him for limited imagination
making a long drawn out chorus
of the world's cramped voice

chastise the bird for breaking up
our neighbor's marriage
with the annoying yap of his words.
It is a lean proposition
getting the canary to do what you want.

Our neighbor resents the interference
your know-it-all attitude over his canary
his marriage, his house
resents the absence of his wife
the way she slips out in the red Mazda
covets more than tidy peonies
a spotless sermon.

The weight of things

you let the poor, outcast
down on their luck
find a home
arrive back late from places
a bus won't carry you.

Street children rub their bodies
along the spine of your upholstery
my mother spreads tomorrow's
breakfast over the table
waits up hours to hear
the soft thump of your steps.

To kiss you must she turn tame
every lusty finch banished
from her body's fruit tree?

Lunar New Year

At the time of the Lunar New Year
you fold white paper into cranes
anoint my plate with an ancient text

toss rice over the wedding couple
golden thread into the broth
with your fish heads

send my mother into the street
with bowls of noodle
almond cookies, paper money
good luck wishes for every door.

Sermon

You drown out my words
ease my mother's voice
into a sermon of your own making

till I am the clear slate
stalked by a blue pen
elope with white cake
the hard mahogany of church pews
a willing wet grave.

Nobody seems to notice
my sheen and buff
body's thin stick
the secret way
I let your luminous
your rain
eat me.

Part Two

When The Sumac Arrives On My Lips

Famine

You moratorium greed.
We get no new shoes for Easter
learn anything can be stitched
in place with enough grit.

My mother is praised for her pluck
the way she salvages pocked apples
heaps of potato for the soup
makes every mud puddle
into a wade pool
holy river calling.

You coral the maimed, lost
my mother's shapely legs
daredevil annoyances
lay to rest the rough and smooth
in a flat bed

till I promise to be everything
angel food cake
the flawless prayer box
salvation of the poorhouse
genuflection of so many shoes.

Sacrifice

I've been trained to
turn the other cheek
seal my fate
the way some folks seal windows

have been pummeled into shape
snipped into deft cotton
till hot coals barely leak out.

But is it problematic
shotgunning crows
as if their goodness
has failed them?

Tease

You are a tease when it comes
to selling train tickets
sending us off to places
we never wanted to go.
Years ago on a mid-winter
train ride to Savannah
I first ran into you
unburdened my soul.

You turn the stubble field
boarded up house
derelict town
into a new kind of scenery

stall me in strange places
for countless days
waiting the length
of your new itinerary.

Your vows

carry a forest
magnificent creatures
instruct the night to send
no army of hailstones.

I am your daughter
first by my birth
second by the loyalty
I give back.

My mother looks on
with her blue organza
struck by the luster of you
way I auger your words
without breaking.

Longing

The ground sucks up mud
sunken petals
the pleated skirt
of my catholic uniform.

I rehearse your love as
a communion table that denies
the extra serving of bread
shrink warps God in a bug jar

in the confession box
recite Hail Marys
beg mercy to remove
its crimped veil.

When *You Make My Heart Swoon*

starts playing on the radio
you abandon your blunt knife
plate of apple
kick off your shoes
waltz my eight-year-old body.

Spawned from my mother's
ballroom of rouged stars
I am reluctant to let her voice melt
carry your chorus
the practiced lilt of your hymns

want to lounge in the seedbed
of some wider foresting.

Pulpit

An insomniac
I walk the shine off floors
sneak sausage
from a sleeping fridge

am learning to cleave
to your chalice
choir boys
the weight of your words
drink gall from the same cup
pocket heaven
like some children
pocket prizes

want to become
your best experiment
recipe for good bread.

Suction cup

We'd crawl out of bed
to the smell of fried eggs, bacon
my mother's hands moving
inside the shade of your flame.

I am your only girl child
the one who aspirins the dark
fabricates blue gentian
mute canaries
sausage that escapes from the bread
welcomes you home with
paper sheep, feathered notions

while you suction cup my past
with your flashlight burning
refuse to take *no* for an answer
dig me up like a tomb robber
out of every grave.

Altar

In church my father
shields his bald head
under a grey fedora
wears a cheap suit
culled words
in case God is listening.

My mother moves out past
the church pew
tilts men's heads to angle
a better view
of her shapely body

this other altar
some live by.

On a clear day

the cat never gets mauled
my father's one hundred job envelopes
yield a willing employer
decent work hours
union pay.

On a clear day
cockroaches stop invading our kitchen
the neighbor next door resists the
impulse to chainsaw his fruit trees.

On a clear day
my father stops feeling useless
gets pampered inside
the world's gift wrap
marked with a decent fate
my mother basks
in her continent of curves
the solace of his pawing.

The earth sings.
They go arm and arm
into the newfound bed of poppies
I have prepared for them.

Spotless

Hemmed in with numbers
probability factors
we never let uncertainty
rattle its broken glass
over our head
babble and burst
through the lack of things
wear our white buck shoes
portrait of you burning.

I attempt to squeeze myself
into polyester
a cramped wish list

sidestep dirt
the messy cat box
crimp disaster
till it bleeds.

You send our prayers skyward

marvel at the way they gather
sun, wind, snow
into a pillowed landscape.

My mother has beaten the cancer
rises from the church pew
in her merle coat
lets you place the host on her tongue
watch her grown back curls
bob up and down the aisle
thankful.

But if poverty has foresworn us
as her bride
what will we do
when more rains come?

Come autumn

you travel groceries to our neighbor
chop wood, stack kindling
warm the kitchen.

We are your prized offspring.
What we know about life is a limited thing
two towns wide, a field of timothy
the distance from home to school
the supper table's soup ladled homilies.

You are the rapt musician
gifter of song
let the cat, the plate, the plow
night sky speak.

Epistle

Your hands are afternoon epistles
aged cheese
heavy pumpernickel
a pinch of paucity towing.

I stuff envelopes
the way pimento gets stuffed into olives
men sometimes stuff their bodies
inside women
blind and indiscriminate
the way some people get stuffed into
a meaningless job, life
must settle for the meager.

You survey my progress
what I have, have not learned
the way I fold and seal
the open white fly
of your limbs.

In a bid to please you

I get pregnant five times
but only one of them
ends up a live birth.
My sadness is eased by the
promise of this child
later the four-year-old sister
I will cross an ocean to hold.

You impel me to taste and test
make a world peopled in gentian
spawn goodness out of my own limbs.

I fold newspaper into cranes
that land in my daughter's scrapbook
where divorce never happens
families stay paper looped in place
with your protective shield.

You threaten

to wreck the car
I've been driving
purge my apartment
the mock happiness
I tack to my door

are a missionary outpost
man who can turn slush
inside the gutters
of the world's gaze

deal in castoffs
the blued body
buried in concrete
moon's shrapnel.

I turn hoarse
voicing your name
bruised sunset

want to spin
dangle in remnants
of my mother's starlit body.

Fallen cathedral

You pronounce parasites
in my kitchen
say they avenue
my fallen cathedral
implore the worker bee in me
to stop lounging.

It is almost Easter.
The sky shakes down
dwarf apples.
I imagine the moon
spilt over the river
a lover so durable
they cleave to the less of me
refuse to condemn
the half-sung nature
of shaved trees.

PART THREE

The Tyrant of Black Beetles

You swallow the crow

scavenge trees
the yard's fruitful.
Our cat isn't happy
feels deprived of her meal.

My mother shrinks under
the weight of your words
way you sermon the sky
flap want
inside the folds
of her nightdress.

You wear your brown beret

have sympathy for other men in berets
who feel they must camouflage
the bald of their head

don't swoon inside the retinol
of literary jargon
keep Rimbaud, Holderlin secret
under the sheen of your lips
palette a world weary pointillism
with insistent strokes.

You succor the birds in the tree
fuel the glass jar with a squadron
of black beetles
sizzle the hell out of them
with the scald of your kerosene.

You go around in cutoffs

help the paralytic find a home
offer up curative versions of faith
designed to save me.

I yank mats out of my hair
worry you'll ask for more
than I can give
cake batter my days
till I am stick thin
can be hoisted up
into a petted landscape.

April arrives.
The rain turns into tulips.
No one notices them mapping
their decay at my door.

Grey flannel

I've been trying to get inside
ambush your thoughts
the world's penitentiary.

You spill the sun in my shoes
offer up morning bun, coffee

call me *dreamer*
the way I slumber with stars
sidestep celebrity

nail my voice to poems
that host the day's
least certain homilies.

A preacher in worn shoes

You sit at the plank table
under the box tree
let ants travel you
stir worship
into the ordinary crust
of our bread.

The ants lift
honor your voice's blue faucet
erect a twig podium
birch bark seats

proselytize beetles
thirst for them
multiply like a season
of dark eggs hatching.

You bolt the house shut

pray for me
as if I am the derelict child
cancer patient
wobbly boat thrust into
a gelled ocean.

Sunday speaks in tongues
of praise
resurrected honeysuckle.

I am stunned, derailed
divined, blessed.
My mother ladles soup
succors the outcast of me
goes miles to beg worship
to unbind its thick veil.

Hail Marys

We have been known to sling stones
prostrate birds, fire hydrants, puddles
the man who walks down our block
tilted as a fallen Jesus
have been known to detonate
what we don't understand.
My mother's prayers follow us
her *Hail Marys,* blue rosary.

When we grow up
will we become shiny as neon
alphabetical rooms
the computer with its multiple
windows humming
learn not to openly throw sticks
but dazzle like cat eyes
proselytizing winter?

Father

I know your orphaned past
dead mother
stumble from school to school
the way being cast out
can anchor with a harsh fist

know your fierce words
practiced attrition
how I'm being admonished
to offer up an alpine voice
unstuck meadow

while the chipped moon
casts her pearly maul
over my damp treatises.

I am unable to understand

this stalwart god
embedded in the priest's sermon
that breeds compliance, thick walls
forges my faith into something
no fatter than a chalk stick.

My mother doesn't want to be
a fallen continent, beggar of kisses.
Thirty years old and still a servant
of wind, summer's rapt tutelage.

When she walks down the church aisle
I know there is another room
and that your Jesus alone
may not save me.

Back then

You rarely danced
held my mother's lips close
twirled her kitschy yellow body
like a spark of the dark playing.

We dined on repentance
a scarcity of shade
the forecast of a world
gone crazy.

Over the years her voice
turn into spooned tapioca
plastic flamingos
a pocked flame.

Hydrant of psalm

My mother is a hydrant of psalm
on a windswept day
chastises the less in me
way I eat with a strict spoon
stickpin happiness
to a budless vase

props me up with tales of
wolves, rabbits
girls who jump over flame
again and again
live to tell about it.

You impose your hands
over her roses
turn the room mercury
till we are the house with a prophecy
of the world breaking

I am exiled from both kingdoms
I once called home.

Stranger

You kiss the house goodbye
till I am a stranger at my own door
girl convinced no man can save her.

I listen to the ache of things
unsung roads
companion my day with
swamp grass, silence
borrowed shoes
keep my nothing
married to your flame.

Crows collect at the table
dark bread
the petals of how many
periled summers
I want to save.

Blue chastening

You come to me with
armloads of wood
blue chastening
white panty your love

while our myrtle
offers up her own
wet version of holy.

I want to become the girl
unafraid of seduction
hazardous words.

Is it easy to walk on stilts
sidestep the ceremony
of the rain's aching
make a strict procession
of the sky's wish list?

Ringing

You are a swollen bell
dangerous lover
furnace of flame.
There are countless reasons
to ignore the tone
of your ringing.

The treasonous girl
in a clashing red skirt set
I am afraid of polished rooms
banners of victory
puddles with a shiny voice.

It will take more than a cubbied heart
stubble of chocolate
bell ringing
to unearth the miracles in me.

But am I melting slow
very slow
inside the drip of your flame?

Premature bride

You think our courtship is over
have sent out the invites
purchased a black tuxedo
as if I am a rollover
trust what comes to me
via a box of chocolate
foil kisses

but I resist your sweet talk
that exiles uncertainty
reduces my mother to just a caged canary
suffragette longing for lace.

Am I the premature bride
who must claw her way
out of the might of things
till your fire and brimstone
can lounge in the rough
the smooth of me
till I am the girl
pampered by fig trees
a decent surplus of dates?

My father trophies the dead

the praying mantis in our yard
fries beetles in kerosene
burns the bane out of things
till heavy with surety
our vows stick to his plate.

I hive penance, hero worship
hide the knowledge in my head
follow his recipe for perogies
strudel, pine nuts with chevre
the precise caramel custard

rise up on tiptoe to spy
the moon beyond the fence
my mother's secret
stampede of cosmos.

Part Four

The Sky's Least Certain Homilies

Half sung prayer book

Are you the seducer
who loiters my dreams
till I am the wind's whittled sister
guttural chant
a half sung prayer book?

God grants even the least of us
some serenity
that was my mother's consolation.
She foraged for the small in things
met dissolution with a star struck gaze.

Tell me again
is it problematic to shotgun birds
as if their goodness has failed them?

Torn places

Do you have me fraternize
with the lack in things
so I can become a lover
of torn places

see through pain
dissolution
clear to the center
and into the darkest room

spike heel my past
into a sequined
deathbed?

It was the moment of shot gunned glass

a bullet hole in our neighbor's pot
reserved for orchids
his screen door plastered in three places.
Now our neighbor has bolted his house
erected a metal fence
no longer lets tulips disturb
the concrete of his drive.

You and the neighbor have grown apart
don't have words for it
no longer chat, share coffee
let an indeterminate moon find space.

Later, my mother gets yanked from life
with a heart attack nobody sees coming
our neighbor moves away.
I tether to the want in things
watch you drown in a sea of job applications
too many bills
pray to a different father who plants
paper crane, quiet miracles
unmines concrete.

In the version I plant in my heart's closet
my brother stays in college, finds a life
never lets crack hound the hell out of him
you get health insurance, a decent job
let the beetles co-exist with the yard daisies
my mother doesn't die

paints her canvases in a torrent of flame
is pursued by lovers who kiss
the complex sums of her
don't turn away.

In my version
the world appreciates shy words
slow things
our neighbor forgives the past
its tainted rooms, overripe melon
decides to plant his parlor windows
in amaryllis.
Come winter we marvel at the
sprays of white blossom they hold.

You wear your bangle hat

over the moon's loose tongue
threaten to mark fear
cancel out the apostrophes.
I sacrifice the voracious spoon
for a scant plate.

Am I rock piling my way
toward heaven on shaved knees?
Will my mother's territorial
gaze over the roses
turn perfunctory?

Time wears on.
I grow up, grow down
begin to handhold the past
lean a soft back
over my mother's trellis.
Decide someday I will marry her.

You tire of plaguing my head

with your words, want to win me
with a new tune
bric-a-brac on the walls
indirect flirtation
flocks of geese unperturbed by
the prospect of wintering
speak in the drunken retinol of hope
while Jesus saves.

I arrive to speckled eggs
paper cranes hatching.
Lightning bugs nibble the dark
lantern my hands silver.

If you were a young girl

maybe you'd spend yourself
till nothing was left
but the horses in the field
buckled shed
roma apples spilling themselves
willing onto the grass

you'd strut around in baby dolls
lick summer ice
absolve the rain for looting.
No shoes would be too big
too small for you.

If you were a young girl
I might be able to speak easier
break into pantomime
halt the stomp of death in my bed
relearn the hushed language of roses.

If you were a young girl maybe
I wouldn't need to become somebody
could pause inside meadow, stream, stone
street urchin homilies
the day's amber hold
over my body's fluency.

I was wax winging

the night's incessant hold
when you stepped in
provided a way station
where what barely survives
can find a stake, $20 room
styrofoamed coffee.

Afterwards, I start singing
jazz tunes, gospel
turn fugitive wants into verse
watch the rabbits in my field
carve a home.

I may be the least of your homilies
yet still you hold a place
travel my soul.

My mother

stores up heirloom pages
saucy dresses
peaches and pestilence
the aeronautics of space
on thrifty wheels
refuses to let remorse eat her

salves my words till I can
ammunition the past
will back wounded animals
a bird's feast table
unman the light that's been
looted.

PART FIVE

You Want to be a Troubadour

A troubadour

You sing ballads below my window
invite me to come out, listen.
Your voice is shaky, the earnestness
of your sentiments are not.

Beyond a world of cynics
you woo me on the soft chorus
of yellow roses, poems
till my skirt starts to fit

every vineyard I pass
becomes an arbor
swamped and stained purple
with the weight of your fruit.

Kisses

I wake to a plate of eggs
the man in my life
estimating wealth
want to be the choir box
of your fiercest longing.

You wield your voice
crushed petals
kisses so durable, insistent
they wake up the snow.

I spread compost
offer up the grove
of my thin trees
for the eye of your foraging.

There is the promise of spring

early crocus
feckless girls squired by deer
peeled words, thimbleberries
the dogs racing through timothy.

I bake sloped loaves of cornbread
call them *gift*
clear the path to my door
let you speak to me
in the language of camisole
complexity, dark loam.

The future pries itself open.

Devotion

I conspire with fate
watch the ivy worship
then strangle our trees
slugs exude their
messy devotion
watch your sweet peas
rise up
a perfect swell
of pink homilies.

When you map
your hands in me
is it the wind's salt tongue
death spiral of leaves
cluttered field given back
to the farmer's mercy?

My past with its pinholes
periled rooms
lets the light seep
starts to handhold the rain.

You bring morning tea
pale toast with honey.
My ordinary shoes
turn luminous
in the cup of your gaze.

An inventor

You clutch hair brained schemes
break up the world's diligence
with the wave of your stick

reclaim misshapen shoes
the boy burdened with bricks
dissolution that can lurk beneath
a woman's housedress.

I squish and squirm
mark my body
like earthworms
in the dark broth
of muddying

swim inside
the wobbly dark pool
of your gaze.

In my dream

you reinvent your life in me
counter the impulse for money
with the green of your cake
cure my lover's lips
till he can taste my resin
the hum of cedar, balsam
stop closing down
like a treatise that never comes
broken homily

in my dream you blow kisses
into a blue basin
encourage me to taste and test
the elsewheres
that are left to me

till I am empty
can hold any mean
or sentient thing
without breaking.

It is hard to believe

you could move in like this
disarm rooms
corner my past
so it doesn't speak cruel.

My mother comes up for breath
in her blue zipped ocean
fields mercy into the
floating realm of my bed.

I begin rowing toward Eden
in my leaf mulch boat.
Stall at the edge of your voice.
Learn to stand still as a tree praying.

Part Six

You Ask the Dark to Speak

When they amputate your bad leg

you learn to lean your weight
on the opposite side
tilt like a misguided missile
popsicle sucked heavy on one end.

Sometimes it is painful watching you
work hard to get up
balance a tray table of ravioli
beg the pace of the world to wait.

The doctor talks about fitting you
with a new prosthetic
one that almost matches
the original shape, color of your leg
lets you travel in ordinary shoes
uncut pant legs.

You ponder the marathon of things
climbs up Mt. Bachelor, Rainer
the Three Sisters
being married to rugged soles
the instruction manual of the world
till it claims you.

They have amputated your bad leg.
You go around on crutches
dally with children, flowerbeds

the slow assaults of the rain
work with your crutch to find the world
more than half of what it's measured to be

in summer
spawn purple cones
siren the foxglove to spire
gather the silt of certain affections
the absence of one bad leg brings.

In the hospital

you are a lousy patient
threaten to streak out
to the nearest burger joint
gulp down a shake with fries

don't like antiseptic rooms
doctors with stethoscopes that track
the sinister or salvation
glue hope to a tape measure
prefer Ella, Gillespie
Nat King Cole, your dead wife
the sweetgrass calling

refuse to view life as a bug jar
without many holes
hoist yourself up out of bed
plot a way to weave my life
into a final bird's nest
of your own making.

Levitation

You levitate women
children, poems
paucity and trees

sorrow over
the scant of our gaze
way things get bullied.

I wonder at the pure
magician of you
way you vanish
what you will later
claim.

New bread

I watch the world's
mock prosperity
carefully timed eggs
toast and suet
anguish that lurks
behind every spoon.

Will you hound my heart
till it doles out new bread
turn my nothings
into something
along the dark corridor
of your rails?

When we ward off

the heart's ice pond
gaze beyond the parking lot
into your patchwork of fields

listen to the earth's voluptuous
don't be too sure
our dark will untangle

we'll recognize easy
the ruby of your clover
this other dimension waiting.

Your heart is a cobbled mill

turned out to pasture
project for a downtown mall
where artisan bread, frothy drinks
overtake the thick of
old brickwork.

When I drift off
amid the world's confusion
muddled dictionary
it is hard to know if you are relic
reclamation project
or just the lost sound of incessant
looms clicking.

You wear a kilt

want to play the bagpipes
but your fingers aren't willing
have a habit of going off to cup
the rounded curve of the fruit

are too old to be cavorting around
with your pleated skirt
stories of the old country
small folk
dining on plates of herring
surfeits of ale.

You wander the lawless roads
in your green tartan
scud your boots through bog country
lend tales of resurrection, ship wreck
to the sprawl of a pub booth
mahogany stain of the pews.

For periled creatures
offer up a sling bag of hope.

Part Seven

The Afterbirth of Attrition

When your sumac grazes my lips

I embark down an ancient river
wedded to sky
summer's rapt tutelage of roses.

When your sumac grazes my lips
I swell in the pulp
blood red juices

finger my summer dress
the orchard's love of decency
smooth skinned belly
of the pear.

The chef in a pampered kitchen

You are a plum catch
whisper of Rilke
conquer my torn hands
with the flirt of your mint.

No longer afraid
I eat the suet crust of your pastry
fuse my life to the taste and test
of your spoons

become hand blown glass
straddling a heat wave
the afterbirth of attrition
threaten to love you sillier
more tragic
more deeply than the rest.

You usher my life

into a door opening
forgive the sullen neighbor
who chainsaws trees
forgive the assault of tarmac
packages that arrive
with an anonymous grin

swoon over my heart's heat lamp
offer up immigrant bread
the resin of paw prints

the soot and silk
swamp and stain
of your pocked hands
for the likes of my foraging.

You run a brew pub for love

concoct potions
come with the silliest names
the lusty sister, petulant pony
incandescent herbal, salient satin
nest me in homages of your own making

till I cleave to your amber tint
refuse to be ambushed by money
wake up the girl in love with trillium
tinctures of hope scattered
across the earth's green platelets.

Hymn

In March I become pregnant
go around in a skimpy dress
obsess over cribs
baby booties, a stroller
space in my bed.

You search my palm
spot the shy girl
floating on crystal
ruby throated hummingbird
green of the world
beyond wreckage.

I wake to your orchard
my mother lifting
out of her deathbed
learn to swim
in your dark water
unafraid.

You stockpile kisses

I clear my throat
make room
court flame, field, bog
the sky's seamstress
become the song box
pressed over every hurt thing
as if the mother of god
is calling

become vestibule
your soft injunction
to nuzzle and lick
let your sunrise
unruly river
claim me.

Pulpits

My mother is a fluid gypsy
elegant crane in her silk kimono
refusal to bow to the petty of things.

In the yard floral sheets wave
her clear eye pulpits the roses
keeps black spot from defaming them.

I am left not knowing
what the future will bring.

Part Eight

A Chorus of Varied Thrush In the Trees

Snow

You court poems, clay, birds
knit longing into the
valley of my purse.

How long have I been rowing
to Morrissa in a cramped boat
mapping loneliness
while the dark speaks
in snow?

I opt for the snow
mounds of it
float on these puffs of forever
that wear your face

no longer go off berserk
chastise the wind
for looting things.

You send juncos into the tree

regrow my stump of geranium
remind me that what's been lost
can come back as the whisper of phlox
summer's field grass.

Deep inside the forest
of my own imaginings
every red gnat
diminutive lady slipper
pulverized being speaks
in the palpable language
of faith.

I used to shrink inside

grey, rain drenched winter
set myself up as a summer dance queen
in love with paisley, sundresses
sand tossed hair
the loose eye of a guileless
sea opening.

But that was before you began
to seriously rehearse your love
frame snow angels in the field
nights so fearless they lure
the moon to my porch.

I have become a storied book
priestess of skunk cabbage
worpsweed, thistle
in January
weave row after row of rag rug
slip into mud boots
rework the scarcity of winter
amber my field with the resin
of your secret burning.

A shy being

I take in your porous
the way you comb thistle
forklift the neighbor's lament
coax purple spires
with the mottled promise
of your voice.

No longer buried under the
weight of the world's pain
every corner becomes spacious
an emblem of what might
become of me.

I spend hours fielding my way
hapless at intersections
consumed by your more
than incidental homilies.

You make room

set table under the elm tree
reach beyond the mind's lit city
navigate our lunch
with the undeterred levity
of your words
load my plate with chard
sweet potato, poems

make room for geese
fox, pig, mustang
invite long life
marvel at their shape, variety
encourage me
to forage your forest

invite the wet earth
my deepest self
to woe you.

You wear your lusty carnation

play the fool
dismiss what we sometimes hoard
leak fireflies, a silvered river
into our recess.

I learn to spell the language of fiddle
lost creatures, a velvet room
forward and backwards
live past the castration of roses.

A troubadour
you wear your lusty carnation
ink the stars, longing
across the jungle of my bed
shameless.

My collapsed orchid
shuns death
gropes her way back
inside your lip's thunder.

You succor the busted
the cankered house, field grass
our gruel as well as our roses
till we can live in the
uneven pause of things
let your kisses
map read the day.

Epistles of light

I start to sing off key
admire the base in things
no longer worry over the way
butter escapes from the bread

become tart and squalor
sweetmeat and thistle
the sky in love with hibiscus
stop denying the surfeit
that has been given to me
slip into my mother's dress
her epistles of light
marginalized landscape.

You festoon the garden
with Queen Anne's lace
bury my body
in her kingdom of grass.

Aerial

We go around buoyant
gather beads of rain
peonies
the loyal plate of cheese
faithful outpouring of the relish

clear our hearts
of their lost pilgrimage
till we can hold paper lanterns
stories and children
words that come out of nowhere
good bread, blue Ebenezer, Caspian Sea
holy wind, sea turtle, treacle
salt kisses, lady slipper

memorize the earth's gift giving
learn to handhold the dark fearless.

You stop being oracular

the reformer of bug bites
dark's spiny skin
let my faded skirt, uneven words
find room in your mission statement

till I am able to dance the tarantula
not drown
become a convent
for my mother's fireweed.

You see past dissolution
pulse your salt stained kisses
across my fragile wing
girlish twirling.

If I can't say goodbye

maybe I can reknit my past
stencil you into moonlight
stay up late night warming
the winter cold in your bones.

If I can't say goodbye
maybe I can refuse to anchor you
to a black velvet mount
the suffocation of bug jars
inaugurate the shrill in you
the petty and pretty
maudlin and scrupulous
gather your fallen leaves, succulence
mysteries that muddy my dark.

If I can't say goodbye
maybe I can refuse to postpone
the daisies at my door
come to you late night
with a new version of folk tale
christen the field, roadway
forlorn places
with a flood of rabbits
the fireweed of her burning.

Easter lily

You arrive with a lily for the meal
are the gracious guest
willing recipient of our bread table
invite the yams, radish, sweet potato
onto your plate, eat slow
recognize the absences we breed
way death can haunt the dragon ware
creep onto a plate.

You hold sway over the garden
your fugitive lusts
decline the slaughter of pig
way greed can swell
shove decency into a coffin

revel in the invitations life brings
admonish me to lick
the fertility of the beets
the arugula, quartered tomato
way they give over their bodies
slide down my throat
willing parishioners
unmaimed by the heavy dark leaking.

Part Nine

*She Crowds Honeysuckle
Into the Pale of My Days*

Since her burial

I am sent to the catholic school
place of grey blazers, strict nuns
trained in contrition
to turn the other cheek
allow goodness, Jesus to save me.
Sundays are tinged with pale wafer
juice washed down
with my secret thirst.

My mother gazes over the world
from the stanzas of my yard
fingers the nasturtium
jewelweed, thistle
lets her body drown
in the pools of water I spray
long and hard
long and hard for her.

My mother had a predilection for kisses

went around in her panties, lace bra
refused to undermine the plush
turned our meals into taste and test
let the saffron, sage speak.

My mother had a predilection for fire
it was planted in our blurred borders
hounded the house till my brother and I
couldn't sleep sensible
and every sermon my father preached
became an act of translation
the garden's timpani
her kiss and tell deliriums
where lust and faith find room
keep us bowered to the earth's
quantum green magnificence.

I want to help

my father know
he is more than invisible
more than a childhood
of spotty orphanages
too many schools

that the trees
with their stalwart devotion
rise up
rise up magnificent
make each precious day
home.

If my mother

corralled me till I could
sit in one place
lull in the shadow of her pear trees
if she could unzip
men's angular sandwiches
words, trousers
calm the bruised children
who rant and rail
in the nest of my ear

if my mother could hoist her hips
around the room's reckless
remind us of mudflats, weed
the yellow canary
lounge her hands in the remainder
of what is left of me
if she hadn't died, shrank

would I be a different voice
a pixie who scallops the wind
grown woman in love with herself
epistolary of generous faith burning?

I make a shrine

for my mother
as if she can be anchored
in one place
with a fist of daisies

am thirsty for her love
have never relinquished
the unworn hope she carries

way she crowds honeysuckle
into the pale of my days
watches over me
a marsh hawk circling.

Exiled

My mother doesn't like letting
an obituary speak
unbricks my path
polishes my brother's buck shoes
till he can see her face.

Spring beetles bathe their
translucent bodies
below our yard table.

My mother doesn't like
letting only an obituary speak
sidles her way in
till we are soulful
a siren of shade trees
past that turns the river
into her psalm.

My mother hairpins hope

staples it to our door.
We know she is dead
but the earth never gobbles
what it takes
sends her back as dwarf chestnut
petals of camellia.

I coin laundry your love
watch the two of you
lean on the ceremony of roses
fold linen
stir fry the bok choy, scallions
the much in the little of things

tuck the spine of the dark
into my dress
thread what remains
beyond dissection.

Part Ten

*The Flock of Birds
in My Bed*

Come April

you take up spring's constituency
bathe in the stream
start to notice the ample
left in the little.

I slowly become the girl
with no flood marks
an invisible kind of foraging
cloak the day in a silted
version of cake

loiter the field
language of deer print
yearning
no longer resist the world's
bird spackled kisses.

My father wants to preside

over my wedding
give me away along the path to the spring
when the time is willing.
It will be mid-afternoon on a brilliant day
the sun loyal as my mother's love.

She wants to witness my clearest nuptial
remembers the girl of my youth
squat among the bee colonies, June bugs
unafraid to soot her skirt.

It will be a long processional.
My two cousins have agreed to play fiddle
the town clerk will loan us her keyboard
crystal punch bowl.
My little brother will make faces
anguish over the velvet knickers
being forced up over his legs.

I will be the girl lifting
so high you can barely contain me
the kisser of trees
emissary of the bird's mating
will rise up so tall I find levity
hold the one I love
nibble you like a perfect cluster
of grapes peeling.

I was once a product

of street malls, attrition
a dice rolled past
camouflaged bread at the table.

Now I wake to a field of rabbits
succulent prayer book
sunrise of geese.

My mother holds her flame
in my heart
whispers of rosemary
columbine, thistle.

Tyrants turn into beekeepers
the earth's sod shoes
a climate of what we gather
what we gift.

My father has divorced himself

from the sting of things
makes a sanctuary of the
dark's latent symphony.
My mother doesn't die
need to do hat tricks
to earn her way to heaven
is welcomed with a filial gaze.

I pearl and stitch
make my lover a scarf
worth traveling in
map his body with my paw prints.

My father has divorced himself
from the sting of things.
Poems arrive
beekeepers, a shy sister
kisses with no tacks.

Shipwrecked, buoyed
accosted, blessed
I become the steady rhythm
of your waves breaking.

When his sketchy past

no longer threatens
my father abandons
the orphanages in his head
fire and brimstone homilies
settles down to the salt
of my mother's kisses
stars traveling a river of fish.

Weaned on the forward elbow
of their love
I give up my lonely forage
into the less of things.

It is March.
Spring threatens to take hold
I am dizzy with blue sky, lilacs
the prospect of flirting.

Pear trees

I let hope find her lost sister
nibble my past
impulse to stir serpents
into the bath water
drown in the afternoon
of your pear trees

by evening
am a dark continent
tropic of rain forest
the ambiatropa plant
that oozes ruby liqueur
out of the green snarl
of her spine.

Grapes

You lounge in the hammock
your body so slight
I am afraid you will perish
if I don't mind your substance
seed you in a tray table of grapes
decent pie.

The slugs are at work demolishing
the lettuce bed, spinach
the day in love with itself
the humming of the bees
séance of napping.

I could sit on the grass
beside you till nightfall
listen to your breath
face's river of stories
tease the arms of the trees
into opening.

Secrets

It's June, wasps plague
praying mantis forage
the fire season is not blind.
I anchor petals to my skirt
a fallen continent.

Almost handsome
my father listens
holds room in his heart
for weeds
the slumped meadow
flouncy roses

no longer resists
the silt in my heels
way I speak in apostrophes
begins to marvel
at the host of secret birds
I feed.

You worship

green nubs of crocus
coyote, wind, weed, snake
children, old people
nurse the dirt's promise
of new life
conspire with none of
the brevity we lend

coax my stalks
to grow thigh high
cradle moist soil
a bundle of wide roots.

The coral barrettes

in my mother's hair
are a sign of your love
shine like waxwings
proselytizing a summer pond
your jeweled faith.
She holds court over the peonies
digs up garlic
with the twist of her trowel.

You have laid table
for lunch under the elm
slice lemon, pickles, bread
cheese to fit the size of her mouth.
Before the afternoon is over
she will claim more than the
bread and cheese from you.

I am your spark of firecracker
on a windless day
the fragile interloper
moth drawn to your light
fused to the delicate span
of your joint wings flaming.

Yellow carnations

You woo my mother on Carolina sunsets
sweetgrass, yellow carnations
the uneven flame of your wick.

She lets you become the lover
she has barely known
lounges in this other wealth
you cast over her bed.

Come spring the two of you handhold
anoint the apartment, modest meal
finch in the tree
tag games, dogs, children

ambition rain or sun
to stay faithful
to every moment
that arrives.

Formosa

You pick the garden's formosa
not for me
but as tincture for my mother's hair.
She lets the best of you bleed through
abandons the rest.

It is March, a time when sin vexes
people disavow meat, sweet tarts
in homage of Lent.
We ambition to fly into the sky's blue coat
pin resurrection to our shoes.

My mother shines my brother's loafers
combs the knots out of my hair
wedges lines of plums plaint as
milky nuns into the kitchen pastry.
The heart tattooed on her arm bulges purple
beneath the sun's blistering.

I am stockpiled, pummeled, gusseted, blessed.
Hope runs ramrod through every corridor.
We squirm and chaff, leap and sing
through chapel service
begin to eat more than the heels of the bread.

My mother speaks the litany of lilac
table talk of tomatoes ripening.
Are we her Lenten mission
browned out jasmine, fledgling forest
the stump trellis of your most succulent roses?

Pampering

I mix grated cheese, ricotta
nasturtium petals, tomato
into the lasagna I will bake.

It is late March, the rain slants
steep as some people's houses.
You are wearing your sultry t-shirt
the one pregnant with holes
fraternize with the less of things
make the old and odd
an orphaned home.

I am suspect of calculated words
unsworn to forsythia
ones that gamble with fate
buy and own, squeeze love into
a jury box, cut glass future

want to pamper you
shadow in your wider decency
leave room
for the sloped lives of women
my mother's singing
the soft winged
holy constituency of her gaze.

Consolation

The woman whose eyes
hold a sirened sea
green boas, forest
knows how to invite me in
offer up a wider version of Jesus.

I become the monsoon
married to missionary shoes
her silvered heat wave

attempt to pronounce
each of my days
with the clear exuberance
of her lips.

It was not how I thought it would be

The homecoming.
My feet were smote
with wormed wood.
When you passed my name
over the candle's flicker
I was afraid it would perish
as a dim thing
sallow curve of naught
in a thirsting heat wave

but it echoed back
rang of my mother's seed.
I was detained, buried, blessed.
My life knelt in dirt
fell apart in your hands.

Now only your beckoning
crawls out of my bed.
You are my weight, buoyancy
fiercest windstorm
palm reader, bee balm
cemetery alongside the roses.

There is nothing I can refuse
shrink from
inside the steady pallor
risen glory
of your arms.

You speak in the retinol of birds

spare no orange or blue dazzle
cast off segregated speech
in favor of the trees
field's punctuated glory.

My mother's skirt bulges with April.
Children turn our backyard kingdom
into a voice box of jasmine.
All afternoon I am reminded of
the loyalties that thread
through the earth's damp tongue.

You are the chatter of swallows
velocity of hummingbird.
I want to pause, listen
paw my way back to decency
shadow the girl who cups hyacinth
lets her body, mud boots speak
mottled as the trunk of trees
luminous inside the secret emissary
of your burning.

Toni Thomas lives in Portland, Oregon. Her poems have been published in Austria, Spain, New Zealand, Canada, England, Scotland, and Australia. In the United States her work has appeared in over fifty literary magazines including *Prairie Schooner, North Dakota Quarterly, Hayden's Ferry Review, the Minnesota Review, Notre Dame Review, Poetry East*, and more. She has been twice nominated for a Pushcart prize, and won several awards. She has published twenty-six collections of poetry and six books for children.

Her figurative clay sculptures have been shown in gallery exhibits in Portland and Chicago, displayed in literary magazines, and housed in private collections in the U.S. and England.

Her short documentary *One of Us* was shown at the Trans-ideology: Nostalgia festival in Berlin and at the Museum of Contemporary Art in Taipei.

Since Toni loves to create and sits buried in reams of poems, manuscripts, clay figures and images….she likes to imagine all of them out in the world swaying wild as the lupine.

tonithomaspoetry.com

www.ingramcontent.com/pod-product-compliance
Lightning Source LLC
Chambersburg PA
CBHW030439010526
44118CB00011B/711